Stuck in the Middle Sea[t]

Why Traveling Can Really Suck!

Observations of a Burned-Out Road Warrior

by: Doug Lipp

Illustrated by:
Vern Mercado

Hickethier Press International

Published by

Hickethier Press International
Fair Oaks, California
1-866-867-1010

Text and Illustrations Copyright ©2008 by G. Douglas Lipp. Registered with Library of Congress
www.douglipp.com

Illustrations and Jacket design: Vern Mercado
                                     www.vernscartoons.com

Layout: Allison Lipp

Printed in the United States of America

1 2 3 4 5 6 MAL 13 12 11 10 09 08

ISBN Number: 978-0-9707648-3-6

Acknowledgments

Vern Mercado. Your unwavering enthusiasm and creative talent is amazing. Your patience and ability to turn this dream into reality is a gift. Thank you!

The speaking bureaus who represent me. I truly appreciate you connecting me with tremendous companies.

My travel agent, Paula McCormish. Thanks for making sure I travel in comfort.

My clients. Thank you for your loyalty over the years. I've learned a lot through our collaboration.

My wife, Pam. You hold the family together during my many absences. Thanks for being such a loving, understanding partner. My children, Allison, Amanda & Keith. You've grown up to be fine young adults. Mom and Dad. You are a constant source of love, support and inspiration.

Dr. Dave Beeman. A fellow road-warrior who shares the pain and shared ideas.

My editors, Elizabeth Coffey and Kirsten David. What keen eyes you have!

My fellow travelers. Some of you are wonderful, some of you are a pain in the backside. Without you, this little book wouldn't exist.

The TSA personnel, flight attendants, hotel employees, airline staff and other travel industry professionals. Thanks for taking these jokes as they are intended ... simply jokes. Your hard work is greatly appreciated!

Note from the Author

I learned a lot about the power of a well-drawn cartoon character when I worked for the Walt Disney Company. Armed with a pencil and an idea, a skilled artist is able to capture any number of emotions in one drawing. Even better, very few words are required. Unfortunately, my artistic skills are limited to stick figures, so I joined forces with a talented, aspiring cartoonist, Vern Mercado, to create what you're now holding.

I am a road warrior. I've been so for 25 years and have experienced every situation in this book, over and over and over again. Odds are you have as well. If not, you will. My hope is that this book gives you an opportunity to escape, through laughter, the challenges of being on the road. My blood pressure actually dropped just by writing it! Whether you are a fellow road-warrior, or an occasional vacation traveler, take solace in the pages you are about to read and realize, things could be a lot worse. So laugh it off!

Doug Lipp
Fair Oaks, California

Stuck in the Middle Seat

Contents

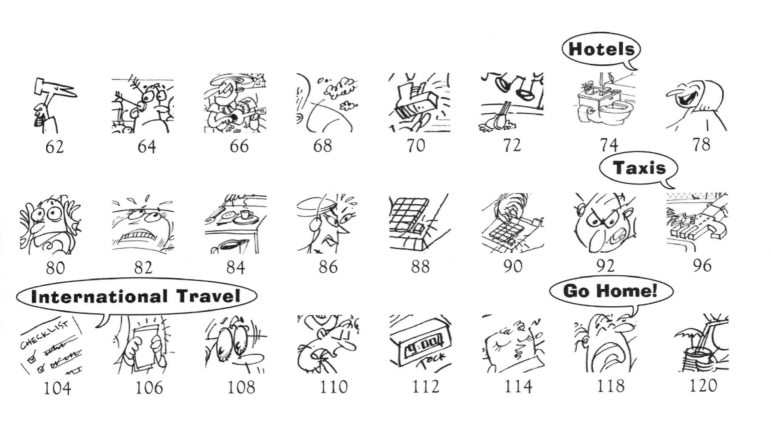

Our Characters

Let's meet our two main characters, Bob
and Lucy. They have been "on the road"
one too many trips and never seem to catch
a break. If you think you're having a rough
time right now, just take a trip with them
and realize
things could be a lot worse...

Our heroes, Bob and Lucy

Traveling Sucks!

"Oh, that's nothing, wait'll you hear my story,
you'll never believe what happened to me...!"

How many times has this happened to you? You're in the middle of telling family, friends or business colleagues about yet "another wonderful travel experience" when someone interrupts to share their own horror story.

Fact: We have all been there and experienced the nightmare of travel.
Fact: Your horror story is better than everyone else's.
Fact: No one really cares what you've been through.
Fact: More is on the way.

That's why you're reading this book. It won't talk back, or try to outdo you. But it will suffer with you in silence and will always be by your side ... as long as you don't leave it on the airplane, in the taxi or in your hotel room.

Let's face it. Traveling can be a major pain.

My hope is that this book will provide you a bit of comfort during your travels. Perhaps it will help you take your mind off what just happened to you ... or what's surely going to happen.

Traveling Sucks!

Traveling, whether for business or pleasure, is demanding. It isn't going to get any easier. The sooner you realize you have no control, the better. Planes will continue to be delayed and flights canceled. You will lose your cell phone or favorite stuffed toy and, sooner or later, your hotel room will be right next door to the ice maker, elevator or, worse yet, the "honeymoon suite." Top this off with a relaxing taxi ride in a big city – plus the joys of jet-lag when traveling abroad, and the package is complete.

Don't despair, you do have control over something ... how you react to all of these wonderful experiences. If nothing else, remember that you have complete control over your own emotions and attitude.

"I know, I know, tell me something new," you say. Well, there isn't anything new on the mental health front. We can complain about what we don't have, fret over what we lost or we can shrug it off and smile. So what if you didn't get your favorite seat, room or meal! You can either let it get you down or let it go. Sit back, relax and take a few minutes to escape in the pages of this book. Have a good laugh, a good cry or just rejoice knowing you aren't the only one who has had so many great opportunities that test your patience.

One more thought ... why don't you go ahead and <u>leave this book</u> on the airplane, in your hotel room, the taxi or bus. It wasn't expensive, and maybe someone else will get a laugh or two.

Flying

If you're old enough to remember the days when we had to "dress up" to go on the airplane, then virtually every aspect of air travel is now maximally challenging. These days, most travelers accept the reality that flying has the same glamor factor as taking a bus.

To get ready for this flight of fancy , please unbuckle your seatbelt, <u>do</u> <u>not</u> bring your seatback to its full upright position, go ahead and keep <u>all</u> of your electronic toys running and, for heaven's sake, please don't hesitate to keep talking on your cell phone.

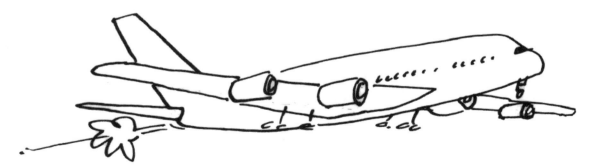

Flying

Let's take a look at some of the more joy-filled events that come as part of the whole air travel package:

- Getting Through Security: *Legalized strip shows in every city*
- Electrical Outlets – Worth Their Weight in Gold: *Didn't we all learn to share in Kindergarten?*
- Pre-Boarding: *"When <u>everything</u> qualifies as a hardship!"*
- Carry-On Baggage: *Take on the most stuff, win the competition!*
- Seating: *Bring your shoehorn.*
- In-Flight Meals: *Take a flight and starve.*
- The Restrooms: *Just hold it!*

- Naptime: *"Leave me alone."*
- Frequent Flyer Miles: *You earned 'em, go ahead and use 'em! Yeah, right.*
- The Best Flying Season: *Two days per year ... that's it!*
- Business or Pleasure: *The definition of "cruel and unusual punishment."*
- Ahh ... Confined Space: *The nose knows.*
- Those !#@!! Regional Jets: *Flying tubes of torture.*

Getting Through Security

Legalized Strip Shows in Every City.

I might be wrong here, but if the
cabaret clubs in Las Vegas,
Atlantic City and Reno aren't
careful, they could lose a lot of
business to the biggest
"stripshow" out there ...
the security checkpoint.

Electrical Outlets -Worth Their Weight in Gold
Didn't We All Learn to Share in Kindergarten?

Isn't it nice to observe so many
examples of "sharing"
when we travel?

Pre-Boarding

When <u>Everything</u> Qualifies as a Hardship.

Is it just me, or does it seem that the
number of passengers who
pre-board ... those who need a little extra
time to board due to
"physical ailments" or age ... has finally
exceeded the number of
regular passengers?

"Step right up, folks. Hangovers, sprained fingers and sunburns <u>do</u> qualify you for pre-boarding!"

Pre-Boarding

Is There no Shame?

I can see it now.
The next rage at airports ...
Rent-a-Granny kiosks.

"We're all together."

Carry-On Baggage/Overhead Storage
Take on the Most Stuff, Win the Competition!

The value of that overhead space cannot be overstated. So, put on your track spikes and sharpen your elbows.

"On your mark, get set ... go!"

Carry-On Baggage/Overhead Storage
Take on the Most Stuff, Win the Competition!

Don't you love those delightful
souls who drag aboard suitcases
large enough to contain a small
nation and still insist,
"It's carry on."

Continued ➡

Carry-On Baggage/Overhead Storage
Take on the Most Stuff, Win the Competition!

Thanks to those bin hogs, many
of us are greeted by some of the
most feared words when we
board:

"We'll have to check your bag, the overhead bins are full."

Seating

Bring Your Shoehorn.

Ahh, stuck in the middle seat ...
enough said.

Seating

You Get What You Pay For.

Nothing like the trip <u>through</u> First Class
to remind us of why traveling
can really suck.

Seating

The Most Valued Inch on the Airplane.

Problem:
Those #!*%#! armrest hogs who actually <u>think</u> it's
a place to rest their arm!!

Solution:
Smile at the hog. Look down at the
hog's arm. Frown.
Sneeze on the hog's arm.
Smile at the hog.

In-Flight Meals

Take a Flight and Starve.

Is it just me, or does it seem like
the airlines are conspiring
to help all of us
lose weight?

Restrooms

Just Hold It.

No doubt about it, airplane designers
are sadistic b_ _ _ _ _s.
How often have you heard this announcement?

*"Ladies and gentlemen, per FAA regulations, please use only those
restrooms in your assigned seating area. For the 5,000 people in
economy, your one restroom is at the back of the plane.
For the two of you in first class, please choose from
one of our 4 luxuriously—appointed models.
Have a nice flight."*

Naptime

Leave Me Alone!

Headphones – check!
Music   – check!
Eyeshades   – check!

Ahhh, naptime ...

Continued ➡

Naptime

Leave Me Alone!

Why do they do this?

"Will you be purchasing a snack box this evening?"

Continued ➡

Naptime

Leave Me Alone!

I've seen the signs that say:
"Seat cushions can be used as life rafts,"
but I've never seen the sign that says:
*"When you stand up, grab and shake the
seat in front of you."*

... Seems like everyone else has.

Continued ➡

Naptime

Leave Me Alone!

Don't get mad ...

... just a little closer ... come on ... a little bit closer ...

Continued ➡

Naptime

Leave Me Alone!

... Get even!

... heh, heh, heh ...

Continued ➡

Naptime

Leave Me Alone!

Now, where was I???

Frequent Flyer Miles

You earned 'em, go ahead and use 'em! Yeah, right.

Flying around the globe on business has countless benefits: growing younger when one crosses the international date line, learning new yoga positions when squeezing into the ample seating and, joy of joys, racking up those frequent flyer miles. Better yet is the wonderful process of using those award miles to book seats for a hard-earned, family vacation ...
What? You didn't know about the restrictions?

"Yippee! 331 days until my vacation, and I can _finally_ make my reservations this morning."

Continued ➡

Frequent Flyer Miles

You earned 'em, go ahead and use 'em! Yeah, right.

There's a reason you have to book one year in advance ...
this process takes time! Also, what ever made you think
that your whole family would be able to fly on the same
plane, much less, next to each other???
Have patience, the fun is just beginning.

"I'm sorry, the only seats <u>on the same flight</u> will cost you an extra 500,000 miles each."

Continued ➡

Frequent Flyer Miles

You earned 'em, go ahead and use 'em! Yeah, right.

What?
You had something better to do
than listen to "on hold music"
for 16 hours?

"... Your business is extremely important to us, please wait for the next available agent ..."

Continued ➡

Frequent Flyer Programs
For Those "Special" People.

Yes, redeeming those miles is frustrating and
next to impossible.
But, don't ever retaliate by taking
a flight on an airline where
you're not a frequent-flyer member ... ever.

"We are now boarding in the following order: First Class, Triple Elite Flyer's Club, Double Elites, then Elites. For the rest of you, good luck ... heh, heh, heh ..."

The Best Flying Season

Two Days Per Year ... That's It!

The key to a hassle-free trip is timing, and it's
never been easier. Due to crazy weather
patterns, holiday schedules, year-round
schools, and fewer flights, there are only two
days left in the year when you can expect to fly
without delays or other surprises ... one in
early October and one in late April.
If you miss either of these days,
you're screwed.

"Ladies and gentlemen, we will be leaving as soon as we get our wings de-iced."

Continued ➡

The Best Flying Season
Two Days Per Year ... That's It!

Flying in January?
No problem!

"Rest assured, we are using the latest de-icing technology,
so we will be departing soon."

The Best Flying Season
Two Days Per Year ... That's It!

Flying in June?
No problem!

"... We are over-booked today and looking for volunteers ... a free snack box to anyone who will share a seat with another passenger!"

Business or Pleasure?

Cruel and Unusual Punishment, definition of:

Flying to a beautiful vacation destination ...
as a business traveler.
Aloha!

"Ladies and gentlemen, during our trip to Hawaii today, we'll be playing loud island music and having limbo competitions in the aisles ... enjoy!"

Ahhh... Confined Space
The Nose Knows.

Forget the peanuts and snack packs,
I wish the airlines would give us
"odor-eater" face masks.

Those !#%@!! Regional Jets

Flying Tubes of Torture.

My darkest, most perverse thoughts come to life on those flying tubes of torture known as regional jets. It wasn't so bad back when they were used only as puddle jumpers and the flights were 20-40 minutes, maximum. Now, they last for <u>days</u>, and the planes are even smaller than before. So, the following is the dream vacation I wish upon that airline executive who originally thought "smaller is better".
Bon Voyage!

"Don't worry sir, your feet will adjust!"

Continued ➡

Those !#%@!! Regional Jets

Flying Tubes of Torture.

Repeat After Me:

Smaller is better, smaller is better, smaller is better,
smaller is better, smaller is better, smaller is better,
smaller is better, smaller is better, smaller is better,
smaller is better, smaller is better, smaller is better,
smaller is better.

"Your rack of lamb ... enjoy."

Continued ➡

Those !#%@!! Regional Jets
Flying Tubes of Torture.

Repeat After Me:

Smaller is better, smaller is better, smaller is better,
smaller is better, smaller is better, smaller is better,
smaller is better, smaller is better, smaller is better,
smaller is better, smaller is better, smaller is better,
smaller is better.

What did I do to deserve this???

Hotels

Nothing can compare to the thrill of anticipating what awaits us behind that door; the absolute rush of adrenaline that accompanies that first peek at our new home-away-from-home.

- Checking-In: *Who trains these people?*
- Room Cleanliness: *Stop! Don't touch anything!*
- Room Service: *Buy a cup of coffee, mortgage your house.*
- The Fitness Center: *No wonder we're all in such great shape.*
- Telephone "Message Waiting" Light: *Want to delete it? Are you sure? Really?*

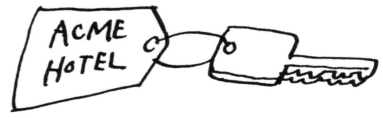

77

Checking In

Who Trains These People?

If you ever find an employee
at the registration desk who knows
<u>anything</u> about the rooms or the
property, pinch yourself.
It is most likely a dream,
and you'll soon awaken to
the nightmare of reality.

78

Continued ➡

Checking In

Who Trains These People?

Sweet dreams!

Room Cleanliness

Stop! Don't Touch Anything!

For your own peace-of-mind, never,
ever give a second thought to all of the
germs and disgusting things
that live on the surface of
everything you touch in your room.
Just ignore the little critters,
and they will go away ...

Room Service

Buy a Cup of Coffee, Mortgage Your House.

The "in-room dining experience."
Ahh, nothing quite like it anywhere
else on earth. Where else can you
spend the equivalent of our national
debt on a cup of coffee?

The Fitness Center

No Wonder We're All in Such Great Shape.

Keeping in shape on the road
has never been easier.
Most hotels now offer
state-of-the-art exercise
equipment in their spas.

Telephone "Message Waiting" Light
You Want to Delete It? Are You Sure? Really?

Ever tried to delete a voice mail
message from your hotel telephone?

"... To delete this message press number 1 ..."

Continued ➡

Telephone "Message Waiting" Light
You Want to Delete It? Are You Sure? Really?

Come on, delete it!

"... You are about to delete this message, to confirm press number 2 ..."

Continued ➡

Telephone "Message Waiting" Light
You Want to Delete It? Are You Sure? Really?

This is where it gets really interesting!

"... Do you really want to do that? Are you sure? If so press
number 3. This is your last chance to change your mind!"

Taxis

Our first impression of the many cities we visit is courtesy of the welcoming-committee-on-wheels ...
taxicabs.

- Maximum Security? No, it's a taxicab.

Taxis

Maximum Security? No, it's a Taxicab.

Let's not pick on taxis or drivers. In addition to transporting us to and from our many destinations in an environment of luxury and cleanliness, they serve another valuable function: They are the models of locked-down, maximum-security efficiency that our prison system should copy.

International Travel

So, you've conquered the domestic marketplace, and you're ready to take on the international scene. First and foremost, don't worry about language, culture, currency or legal differences from country to country. These are minor issues that can be handled by the virtual army of experts out there: Language barriers? Forget it! Hire an interpreter and a couple of translators and you're covered. Worried sick about committing one of those annoying "cultural mistakes" in front of your foreign hosts? (Hmm, was I supposed to burp after the meal or throw my plate against the wall to show my appreciation ???).

Not to worry, there are plenty of culture consultants who will help you keep your foot out of your mouth. Exchange rates causing you sleepless nights? Don't sweat it, international bankers are a dime a dozen.

No, these are just minor irritants compared to the real challenge every international traveler faces. By far, *the* biggest challenge for you to overcome, one that has yet to be conquered by even the most seasoned road warriors is ... jet lag.

International Travel

Think you're ready? Great. Before you make your reservations for your dream vacation, or schedule those meetings at the far reaches of the globe, I suggest you follow the protocol listed on the next page. Do this for three consecutive days *before* finally deciding if you're ready for the rigors of international travel. Make sure you start the first step very early in the morning, well before you would normally wake up. For example, if you normally get up at 6:00 a.m., shoot for a 3:00 a.m. start. Here you go:

First: Pour sand into your eyes, lots of it ... feel the burn.

Second: Swallow several bottles of laxative ...
            get things really gurgling in there.

Third: Repeatedly bang your head against any hard object ...
            start that killer headache.

Fourth: Blow a loud horn directly into your ears ...
            soon, they'll be ringing on their own.

101

International Travel

By now, it will be getting fairly close to the time you usually get up and you will have completed all four steps. Feeling pretty good? Perfect, your day has just begun! Now, without taking a nap, go through your normal day of meetings, carpools, phone calls and e-mail writing. Continue two more days in a row and see how you do. By no means is this a cure for jet lag, it is simply a way to sample what's going to happen to you on the other side of the International Date Line.

Welcome to the joys of international travel, global business and jet lag.

- **Anti-Jet Lag Strategies – Going There:**
  Might as well hire a witch doctor.

- **Jet Lag & Coming Home:** *Who cares if your body says it's only 2:00 a.m., time to get up, welcome home!*

International Travel

Anti-Jet Lag Strategies: Going There.

- All-brownie diet 5 days before departure ... check!
- Drink celery soup night before departure ... check!
- No Bee Gees on iPod ... check!
- During flight, drink only purified mineral water from secret artesian wells ... check!

"All set, now it's off to the airport. Next stop, Paris!"

Continued ➡

International Travel

Anti-Jet Lag Strategies: Going There.

After flying halfway around the world, you're all
tucked in and ready for
a great night's sleep, right?

Don't count on it ...

"I *finally* arrived! So glad I followed my pre-trip strategy; this jet lag stuff is nothing."

Continued ➡

International Travel

Anti-Jet Lag Strategies: Going There.

If only I had a dollar for every
anti-jet lag-strategy I've tried
that guaranteed success ...

"Go to sleep ... go to sleep ... please go to sleep ... 100, 99, 98, 97 ..."

Continued ➡

International Travel

Anti-Jet Lag Strategies: Going There.

Sweet Dreams!

"Our country's most famous landmark is just to your left, get your cameras ready."

International Travel

Anti-Jet Lag Strategies: Coming Home.

Don't worry, your jet lag won't last forever.
After just a few days overseas,
your body will adjust to the local time
and you can really begin to enjoy the trip.
Unfortunately, this usually happens
the day you get to fly home.
If you thought adjusting to the time *over there*
was a nightmare, just wait until
you get back.

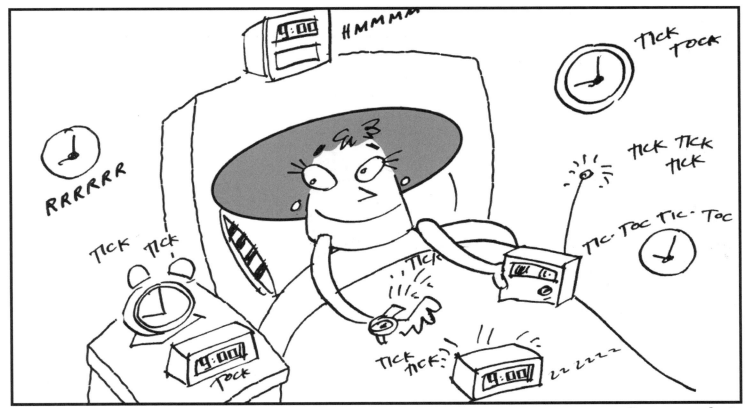

"I just gotta get up in time for that meeting tomorrow morning, these backup alarm clocks should do the trick."

Continued ➡

International Travel

Anti-Jet Lag Strategies: Coming Home.

Welcome Home!

You're Over-the-Top! Had Enough! So Go Home!

You get cranky when your favorite seat on the airplane is taken, you have memorized the layout of every airport in the nation, plus the friendly folks at the security check point call you by name ...
It's time for you to go home.

- What's more valuable than your favorite chair at home? Your favorite spot on the airplane.

- Airport feeling a bit too much like "home?" Get out of there!

117

You're Over-the-Top! Had Enough! So Go Home!
Warning, This Can Happen to Anyone.

You know you're over-the-top when you complain that your "favorite seat" on the plane has been taken. You've turned into a spoiled-rotten baby. Time to pack it in, go home, get over it.

"Whaaa! 7A, that can't be! That's a window and I always get 7C, the aisle seat! Whaaa!"

You're Over-the-Top! Had Enough! So Go Home!

Airport Starting to Feel a Bit Too Much Like "Home?"

You've traveled one-too-many miles
when the following things happen at most of the major
airports. You've memorized:

- The location of your favorite restaurants.
- Which electrical outlets are always open so you can
re-charge your stuff.

– Plus –

- The guards at the security checkpoints and flight
attendants greet you by name.

About the Artist

Vern Mercado

When Doug asked me to join him in this project, I honestly didn't understand the concepts from the manuscript that he sent to me in the mail. Flying, hotels and travel? What could possibly be so funny about that? I rarely travel, but during the process of putting this book together, I had the chance to travel from California, where I currently live, to my home state of Florida. It was then that I understood his humor. Airport security is ridiculous, some travelers are just plain rude and it's really hard to wake up on time in a different time zone. Doug seems to hit all these topics and more and shares them with us in a humorous way. We can laugh "with" Bob and Lucy as we put ourselves in their shoes. We truly feel for them. I've read somewhere that "Comedy is Pain." What could be funnier, or more painful, than following them in their travels? I get "it" now.

Vern is a freelance cartoonist who has drawn for *Mad Magazine*, the *San Francisco Bay Guardian*, and *TV Guide*. He enjoys drawing Web animation and keeping current artwork on his blog. When not drawing, he enjoys taking daily water aerobics classes, quick drives to the Napa Valley and spending time with his wife, Lucille and daughter, Genevieve, through whom he gets all his inspiration. He lives in Concord, California, where he works as a project manager for an architectural firm.

To get in touch with Vern for your illustration needs, contact:

Web site: www.2danimator.com
Blogsite: www.vernscartoons.com
E-mail: vern@vernscartoons.com

About the Author

Doug Lipp

When not stuck on airplanes writing books, Doug can usually be found motivating and challenging audiences around the world as a business consultant and speaker. He is an internationally acclaimed expert on customer service, leadership and global business, with more than 30 years of experience working from the front lines to the boardrooms of corporations around the world. Fluent in Japanese, Doug was formerly the head of corporate training at the Walt Disney University and was on the start-up team for Tokyo Disneyland.

Doug is represented by some of the most prestigious speaking bureaus and agents in the public speaking industry. His keynote topics include: service excellence, international competitiveness and leadership ... and yes, he is known to include many of his humorous stories and examples in all of his presentations.

Books by Doug Lipp:
"The Changing Face of Today's Customer: How to Attract and Retain a Diverse Customer and Employee Base"
"Even Monkeys Fall from Trees: The Balance of Art and Science for Outstanding Customer Service "

To book Doug for a keynote address or place book orders, contact:
Web site: www.douglipp.com
E-mail: info@douglipp.com
Telephone: 1-866-867-1010

All Aboard!

www.stuckinthemiddleseat.com

Join Doug and fellow road warriors as they share real-life travel horror stories, and even a few examples of when things go well!

Doug's *Stuck in the Middle Seat*™ web site is the ticket to helping you cope with another day "on the road."

Submit your own story and if it winds up on the web site, you'll get the credit.

Since your flight is probably delayed or canceled, take time to check out a web site dedicated to you, the tireless traveler!